Girls Can Do Anything!

40 Inspirational Activities

ARCTURUS

ARCTURUS

This edition published in 2022 by Arcturus Publishing Limited
26/27 Bickels Yard, 151–153 Bermondsey Street,
London SE1 3HA

Authors: Anna Claybourne, Claudia Martin, and Thomas Canavan
Illustrators: Ocean Hughes and Katie Kear
Editors: Lucy Doncaster, Kait Eaton, Donna Gregory, Stephanie Carey,
  and Violet Peto
Designers: Lucy Doncaster, Duck Egg Blue, Jeni Child, and
  Sarah Fountain
Art Direction: Rosie Bellwood
Consultants: Dr. Emma Watson, Dougal Dixon, Sarah Ackland, Nina Ridge,
  and Jules Howard

ISBN: 978-1-3988-1989-4
CH010343NT
Supplier 29, Date 0422, PI 00000970

Printed in China

What is STEM?

STEM is a world-wide initiative
that aims to cultivate an
interest in Science, Technology,
Engineering, and Mathematics,
in an effort to promote these
disciplines to as wide a variety
of students as possible.

PLEASE NOTE:
The medical content of this book is
not intended to be a substitute for
professional medical advice. Always seek
the advice of a qualified health provider
if you have any health concerns.

Contents

You Can Be Anything You Want to Be!

Have you ever thought about what you would like to be when you grow up? Maybe you love animals and know you want to be a vet, are intrigued by buildings and bridges and hope to be an architect or a civil engineer, or else you enjoy using computers and plan to be a coder. Or perhaps you aren't sure yet, and want to keep your options open.

Whatever stage you are at, this book can help. It takes a look at a wide range of careers, explaining what the job involves, what you might need to be good at or interested in, and the sorts of tasks you might carry out. What's more, it's packed with loads of fascinating facts and inspirational stories, as well as activities, puzzles, games, and quizzes. The answers for these can be found on pages 90–91.

So, open your mind, grab a pencil and a piece of paper, and prepare to explore the limitless opportunities out there. Who knows—maybe in the future you could be the one to discover a new galaxy, help clean up the planet, or come up with a cure for cancer.

You Can Be an Astronaut

Many kids dream of being an astronaut when they grow up. It's one of the most exciting jobs in the world! You get to see and do things very few other people do, and explore the Universe beyond our planet.

However, it's not easy to become a professional astronaut. You'll have to meet some strict requirements, such as:

- have a degree in a science-type subject, such as engineering, physics, or medicine
- be an experienced pilot who can fly a passenger jet or fighter plane
- be very fit and healthy

Some of the passenger spaceships being developed.

Is there another way? Yes—go into space as a "space tourist." Several companies have developed passenger spacecraft for the future. Tickets are VERY expensive, and you'll have to do some basic training—but not as much as a professional astronaut.

One ticket to space, please!

Activity: Astronaut Quiz

It's not just brains, training, and experience that make a good astronaut. You also need specific personal qualities because being in space can be challenging and scary.

Try this quiz to see how well suited you are to space travel!

1. How do you feel about heights?
A. I love the amazing view from high up!
B. I'm OK, as long as I'm safely strapped in.
C. Help! Get me down!

2. What's your best subject at school?
A. Mathematics
B. Sports
C. Art

3. How do you react in a crisis?
A. Stay calm and look for a solution.
B. Ask someone for help.
C. Run around shouting.

4. Do you prefer company or being alone?
A. I like being in a group and work well with others.
B. I don't mind either way.
C. I need time on my own.

5. How do you feel about small, enclosed spaces?
A. Relaxed!
B. I don't want to be stuck in a small space for too long.
C. Get me out of there!

If you're not ideal astronaut material, don't worry! You can be a rocket scientist, design spacecraft, study space, or lead missions from ground control.

You Can Map the Solar System

However far you travel on Earth, it's tiny compared to the hugeness of space. Even our Solar System is vast. The distance from the Sun, in the middle, to Sedna, the farthest-known dwarf planet, is about 144 billion km (90 billion miles). If you flew that distance in a jumbo jet, it would take you more than 16 million years.

In pictures, the Sun and the planets are close together, so you can see them all. But they are really much more spaced out. The distances are shown on this chart:

The Sun

Mercury—57 million km (35 million miles)

Venus—108 million km (67 million miles)

Earth—150 million km (93 million miles)

Mars—228 million km (142 million miles)

Jupiter—779 million km (484 million miles)

Saturn—1.43 billion km (889 million miles)

Uranus—2.88 billion km (1.79 billion miles)

Neptune—4.5 billion km (2.8 billion miles)

Pluto—5.91 billion km (3.67 billion miles)

Sedna—144 billion km (90 billion miles)

Distances in outer space are often measured in light years. One light year is the distance a zooming beam of light travels in a year. That's about 9.5 trillion km (5.9 trillion miles)! Our nearest star, apart from the Sun, is Proxima Centauri, just over four light years away.

Activity: Scale Model of the Solar System

It's hard to imagine how far apart the planets are, but you can visualize it with a scale model. For example, if the Sun was the size of a soccer ball, Earth would be the size of a peppercorn and about 24 m (79 feet) away!

Put the Sun on the ground, and start walking with big steps, taking the other objects with you. Ten big steps away from the Sun is where Mercury should be. For the rest of the planets, keep walking!

Mercury	10 big steps from the Sun
Venus	Another 9 big steps
Earth	Another 7 big steps
Mars	Another 14 big steps
Jupiter	Another 95 big steps
Saturn	Another 112 big steps
Uranus	Another 249 big steps
Neptune	Another 281 big steps

You will need:

- A big open space, such as a playing field
- An adult to help
- Sun—A soccer ball or a small melon
- Mercury—Head of a pin
- Venus—Peppercorn
- Earth—Peppercorn
- Mars—Head of a pin
- Jupiter—Table-tennis ball
- Saturn—Marble or acorn
- Uranus—Dried pea
- Neptune—Dried pea
- Pluto—Grain of sand or salt

The dwarf planet Pluto can be represented with a grain of salt. You would need to take 242 big steps beyond Neptune to place it on your model.

You Can Be a Rocket Scientist

Think of a rocket, and you'll probably picture something long and thin, with a pointed tip. As all rocket scientists know, rockets are this shape because of drag. It's a force that slows objects down as they move through the air.

Molecules   Air

The air is made up of gases, which are made up of billions of tiny molecules. As an object moves forward, it forces its way through the molecules. These are pushed out of the way and flow around it.

The faster you go, the worse drag gets! To go fast at takeoff, rockets must be streamlined. In space, there is no atmosphere, so objects like satellites don't have to be streamlined.

Airflow

Smooth, pointed, "streamlined" shapes push through the air more easily and smoothly, so they reduce drag.

Wide, bulky shapes push more air aside, making more drag.

Activity: Earth or Space?

Here's a selection of real spacecraft. Some take off from the ground and travel through the air, and some operate only in space.

1

2

3

4

5

6

7

8

Sort out which is which by writing the numbers in the boxes, and then draw your own streamlined rocket.

Draw your rocket here.

Ready for liftoff!

Safe in space ...

You Can Design a Space Base

A space station is a space base that orbits Earth. Astronauts can go to live and work there for weeks at a time. Several different countries have made parts for the ISS and/or sent astronauts to stay.

The Soviet Union launched the first space station, Salyut 1, in 1971. There have been several others since then.

Today, the biggest space station ever orbits the planet—the International Space Station, or ISS. It has been built over many years, by sending more and more sections up into space and attaching them together.

There's space for six astronauts to live on the ISS at a time. They do experiments and study space, as well as exercise and keep the ISS working. More than 200 astronauts from 17 different countries have been to stay on it.

Inside, the astronauts float around in microgravity. There is pressurized air, like in a plane cabin, so the astronauts don't have to wear space suits. There is no "up" or "down."

The ISS has a special window area called the cupola, where astronauts can look at the view.

Activity: Design a Space Station

Space stations are usually made up of tube-shaped pieces. Tubes are strong and one of the easiest shapes to transport into space on a rocket. Check out these space stations, and then design your own below.

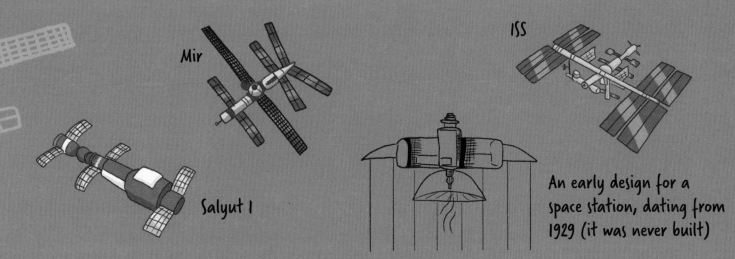

Mir

ISS

Salyut 1

An early design for a space station, dating from 1929 (it was never built)

You Can Be a Multiplication Magician

Learning your times tables in school is something every kid has to do. It's true that they can be really useful (in fact, one of the most useful things you'll ever learn!), but remembering all those multiplication tables can be very tricky. Here are some top tips to help you out.

To make it easier, you just need a few mental arithmetic magic tricks!

For the **four** times table, double the number, then double it again.

For example: 6×4

Double it: $6 \times 2 = 12$
Double it again: $12 \times 2 = 24$

$6 \times 4 = 24$

For the **five** times table, halve the number, then multiply by 10.

For example: 6×5

Halve it: Half of $6 = 3$
Multiply by 10: $3 \times 10 = 30$

$6 \times 5 = 30$

For the **nine** times table, you just need 10 fingers.

Put your hands flat in front of you. In your head, number the fingers 1 to 10. To multiply any number by 9, find that finger and fold it down.

Count the number of fingers to the left of it, then the number of fingers to the right of it.

For example: 6×9
Fold down finger number 6

$6 \times 9 = 54$

Activity: Two-Hand Calculator

In fact, you can use 10 fingers to multiply together any two numbers from 6 to 10. Once you've learned how it works, try it on the questions below . . .

Hold your hands out with the palms facing you and the fingers pointing toward each other.

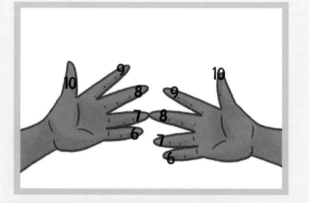

1. Imagine that your fingers are numbered 10, 9, 8, 7, and 6, counting down from the thumbs. To multiply two numbers, touch the corresponding fingers together. For example, 7 x 8.

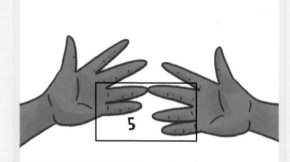

2. Count the two touching fingers and all the fingers below them, and add a zero on the end. In this example, there are 5. Add a zero on the end, which gives us 50.

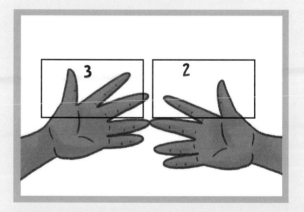

3. Now count the fingers above the touching fingers on both sides, and multiply them together. Here, we get 3 x 2 = 6. Add this to your first number: 50 + 6. And there's the answer! 7 x 8 = 56.

Now use this trick to try these tricky multiples:

6 x 7	9 x 8
8 x 10	10 x 6
7 x 9	7 x 10
9 x 10	9 x 9
6 x 8	6 x 9

You Can Design Fun Fractals

Fractals are a type of mathematical pattern. In a fractal pattern, the same shapes are repeated as smaller and smaller sizes. Have a go at drawing some!

Some natural objects grow in fractal patterns. Look at this fern leaf. Its shape is repeated in each of the smaller sections—and the even tinier sections branching off them.

This is a map of streams flowing into larger streams, which then flow into rivers, which flow into larger rivers. It also forms a natural fractal pattern.

Mathematicians and artists are always coming up with fractal designs and patterns, too. This one is called the Sierpinski triangle.

You start with a triangle.

You add smaller triangles in all these triangles. Now there are nine triangles ...

You add another, smaller triangle on the middle third of each side.

And so on ... and so on.

Activity: Fractal Trees

Many trees grow in a pattern resembling a fractal. The trunk divides into main branches, which divide into smaller branches, which divide into smaller branches, and so on, until there are hundreds of tiny twigs.

Try drawing a tree fractal on some spare paper like the steps on the right.

Then try drawing a whole tree in this space, using the fractal method. What happens if you draw three or four branches each time, instead of two?

1. 2. 3. 4. 5.

You Can Be Great at Graphs

Graphs are a way of showing information in the form of a picture, making it easier to understand and compare facts at a glance.

For example, here's a type of graph called a bar chart. It shows the kinds of pets a group of people have.

You can see right away that cats and dogs are the most popular pets, and rats are the least popular.

This line graph shows how a person's height has changed during their life.

The units on a graph are written along the bottom of the graph (the X-axis) and up the side (the Y-axis). For example, if X = C and Y = 5, the cross shows where the points meet.

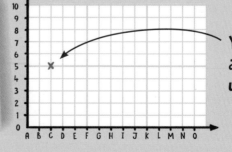

You can mark, or "plot," any point on a graph, using the X and Y axis.

Activity: Graph Dot-to-Dot

Test your plotting skills! Plot these X and Y coordinates on the graph, numbering them all as in the list. Then connect the dots in order. It will make a picture!

Coordinates: (X, Y)

1.	F5	37.	U6
2.	F6	38.	V6
3.	G6	39.	U5
4.	G7	40.	T5
5.	H10	41.	T6
6.	H11	42.	S7
7.	J13	43.	T9
8.	J15	44.	S7
9.	J13	45.	Q5
10.	H11	46.	O5
11.	G10	47.	P6
12.	G12	48.	Q6
13.	H14	49.	R7
14.	H15	50.	P8
15.	G14	51.	P10
16.	E14	52.	S12
17.	C15	53.	P10
18.	D15	54.	P9
19.	C16	55.	M9
20.	C15	56.	K8
21.	C16	57.	K9
22.	F16	58.	J10
23.	G17	59.	K9
24.	I17	60.	K8
25.	L14	61.	K7
26.	S14	62.	M7
27.	W10	63.	M6
28.	Y12	64.	K6
29.	Z14	65.	J8
30.	Z12	66.	I10
31.	W8	67.	J8
32.	U9	68.	G5
33.	U10	69.	F5
34.	U8		
35.	T7		
36.	U7		

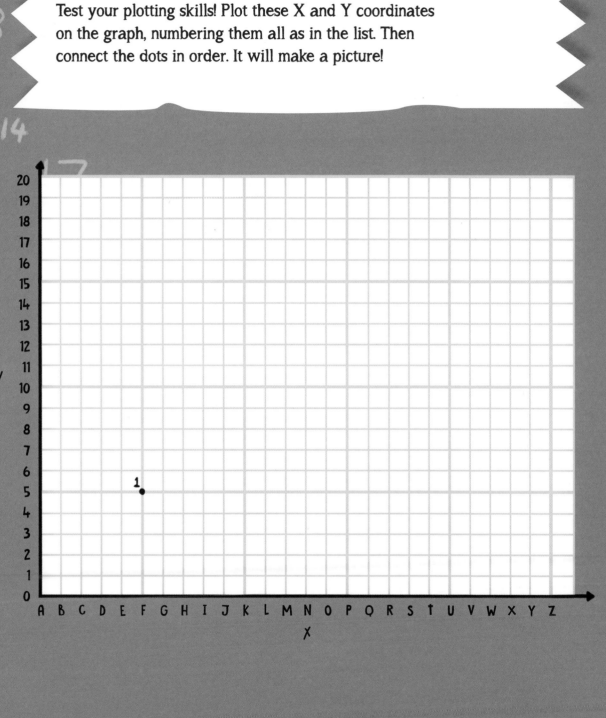

You Can Design a Building

Specialist programs can make many jobs easier. For example, architects use specialist programs to design buildings. This saves time—and lets them be more creative.

Coding software can change the look of a building design in an instant.

Computer programs don't just help architects to be creative—they also help them to test the strength and safety of buildings.

the architect can save different versions of the design, adding or dropping features.

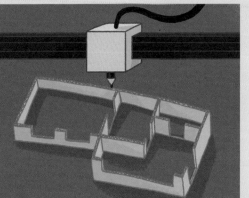

3D printing enables designers to print a scale model of their plan directly from their own computer.

Activity: Building Shapes

Try your hand at some designing. At the bottom of the page are three complete shapes—a circle, triangle, and star. The right code could assemble the orange fragments almost instantly.

See how long it takes you to create the three full shapes from the fragments (a–o).

You Can Crack Computer Code

What begins with basic steps—or simple codes—can develop into a dazzling variety of results. It seems that there's no limit to what coders can manage.

The Curiosity Rover explored Mars—thanks to 2 million lines of code!

We've come a long way since Englishwoman Ada Lovelace wrote the very first computer code—in 1843!

"Imagineering" combines wild imagination with complex engineering—all linked by coding.

Different coding skills come together in the latest video game designs.

Activity: What Comes Next?

Below is a list of coding commands. Another set of commands (a–e) is in a second list. Choose the command from the second list that follows on from each command in the first list.

1. Insert scoop into ice cream tub

a. Print a list of pupils' names

2. Stop vehicle when light is red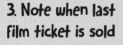

b. Choose a cone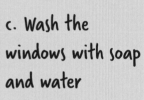

3. Note when last film ticket is sold

c. Wash the windows with soap and water

4. Locate school register

d. Wait for green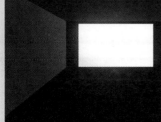

5. Check that car windows are shut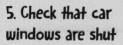

e. Dim lights in the cinema

01101100011010110I
1100101101010011101

You Can Be Brilliant at Binary

Almost anything can be written in binary code, where everything is represented by 1s and 0s—including the 26 letters of our alphabet. Each 0 or 1 in the binary number is called a bit, short for binary digit.

Phones turn sounds into binary code, then transmit the information as waves.

"Smart" TVs and DVD players rely on information stored or sent in binary code.

Much information expressed in binary code (like the alphabet opposite) is made up of a string of eight bits.

Engineers can send messages huge distances to spacecraft and satellites using binary code.

Activity: Decoding a Message

Here is the alphabet expressed in binary code.
Can you decode the message written in this code?

A	01000001	N	01001110
B	01000010	O	01001111
C	01000011	P	01010000
D	01000100	Q	01010001
E	01000101	R	01010010
F	01000110	S	01010011
G	01000111	T	01010100
H	01001000	U	01010101
I	01001001	V	01010110
J	01001010	W	01010111
K	01001011	X	01011000
L	01001100	Y	01011001
M	01001101	Z	01011010

01001001

01000011 01000001 01001110

01010010 01000101 01000001 01000100

01010100 01001000 01001001 01010011

You Can Be a Robot Designer

You can divide robots into different types depending on how they work or move, or what jobs they do.

When robot engineers start designing a robot, they have to think about how it will move, in order to do tasks and get around.

This robot doesn't go anywhere, as it's just an arm for building things in a factory.

If a robot is going to move around on a flat surface, engineers often give it wheels.

Robots with walking legs are harder to design, but they have improved a lot in the 21st century. Some can climb up and down stairs.

Robot engineers have invented thousands of different robots which can carry out all sorts of different tasks. Here are just a few of them ...

There are even swimming and flying robots!

Search and rescue robots find people and save them from danger.

Farm and factory robots do simple, repetitive jobs such as picking fruit.

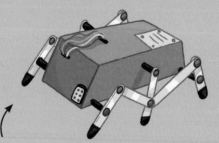

Some robots help with daily life—like this robot that's designed to help you sleep.

Activity: Your Dream Robot

What do you need a robot to help you with? Making your bed, scoring goals, scaring away spiders—or something else entirely?

In this space, design and draw a robot that you'd love to have around.

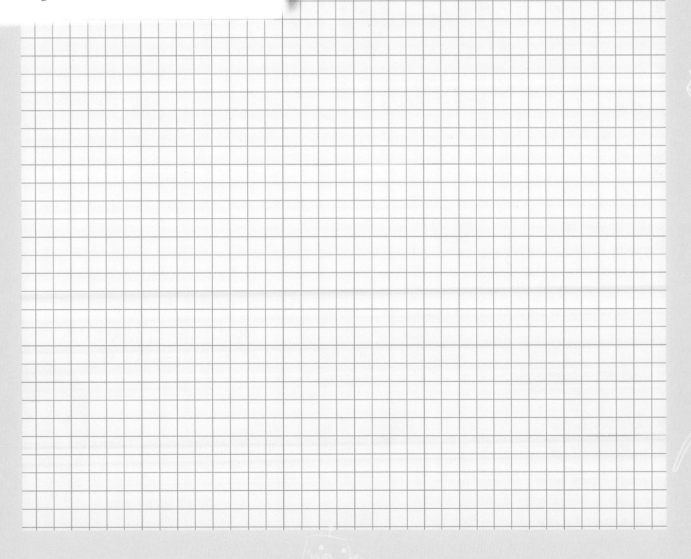

You Can Design Animal Robots

As well as humanoids, robot engineers and designers have come up with all kinds of amazing animal robots.

Different types of animals give robot engineers ideas for new designs and ways to solve problems.

This kangaroo robot copies the way a real kangaroo moves to jump really high.

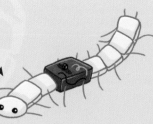

Robot crabs can walk along the seabed.

Snakebots, inspired by snakes, can crawl and slither along the ground, making them good at hiding.

Robot jellyfish move like a jellyfish underwater.

A robot with lots of legs, like a spider or a centipede, is very stable and can crawl over obstacles easily.

A sloth's arms inspired this robot that can move along a rope.

This sloth robot crawls around in a tree, and real sloths come to investigate it. Inside, there's a camera that films the real sloths in closeup.

Nature scientists have started using animal robots as spies, to get close to the animals they want to study.

Activity: Animal Abilities

Here's a selection of animals with different features and abilities. What kind of robots could they inspire?

Match each type of robot to an animal, and draw a robot version of the animal to do the task.

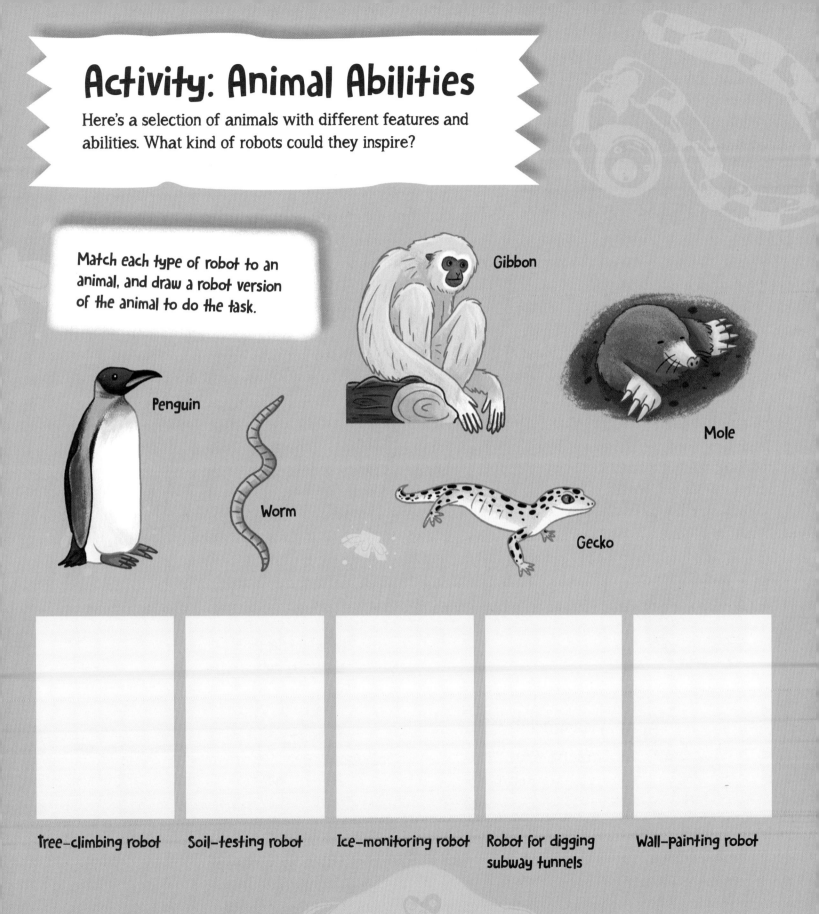

Gibbon

Mole

Penguin

Worm

Gecko

tree-climbing robot

Soil-testing robot

Ice-monitoring robot

Robot for digging subway tunnels

Wall-painting robot

You Can Design Drones

Flying robots are incredibly useful as they can go anywhere. But they are a challenge to design, as they have to be light enough to get off the ground.

A drone is a small flying machine—and a drone with programming and sensors is a kind of flying robot.

Drones fly using rotors, like a mini helicopter.

These drones can join together in flight to make a bigger robot.

A flying, flapping realistic robot bird, based on the shape of a seagull.

Bat bot with wings made of a thin silicone skin.

Beautiful flapping butterfly bots.

Flying robots have many uses, like carrying deliveries, making maps, and testing air quality.

Tiny robot bees could be used to pollinate crops.

Activity: Drone Bot Delivery

This robot drone needs to deliver an emergency first aid package to an injured hiker who's stuck in the forest. You have to program it to make sure it finds its target.

You can use these commands to program the drone. Write a list of commands that will get the drone to the hiker and avoid all the rocks, as they are too tall to fly over.

Commands:

- Take off
- Stop and land
- Fly forward
- Fly backward
- Fly left
- Fly right
- Fly up
- Fly down
- When you see a tree
- When you see a river
- When you see a lake
- When you see a rock
- When you see a log
- When you see an "SOS" sign

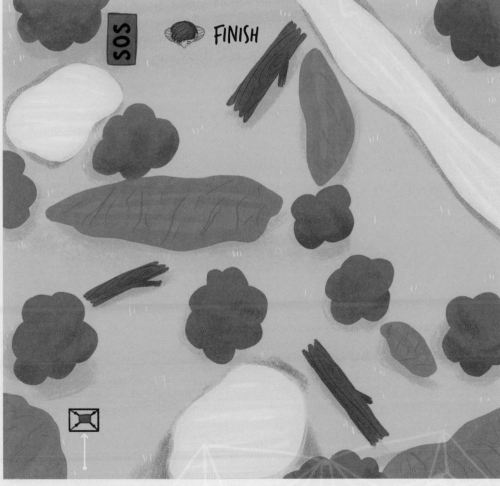

SOS FINISH

START

We've started the program for you:

Take off

Fly forward

When you see a tree—fly right

_____

_____

_____

_____

_____

_____

_____

_____

You Can Be a Civil Engineer

The very first bridges were very simple—just a log across a small stream. Fast-forward to today, though, and we have awesome bridges that cross rivers and ravines.

How did we invent modern bridges like these? How do they stretch across a huge gap, with cars, trucks, and trains driving over them, and still stay up?

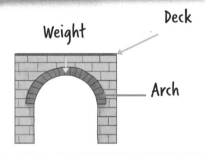

Weight

Deck

Arch

Bridge designers use shapes such as arches to create strong structures.

The Akashi Kaikyo Bridge in Japan has a central single span that stretches 1,991 m (6,532 feet) over the sea.

It is a suspension bridge. The deck is hung, or suspended, from cables attached to tall towers.

Stone, concrete, iron, and steel are strong materials often used in bridges.

Australia's Sydney Harbour Bridge has a single span of 503 m (1,650 ft).

The Sydney Harbour Bridge has a metal arch above the deck. Cables attached to the arch hold the bridge up.

Activity: Design a Bridge

Find out how bridges stay up best, by building some yourself.

You will need:

- Scissors
- Craft card
- Pencil and ruler
- Two empty cardboard boxes, such as tissue boxes
- An every object to use as a test weight, such as a can of beans
- Paper straws
- String
- Tape

1. Cut a strip of card to make your deck, 30 cm (12 inches) long and 10 cm (4 inches) wide. Use it to make a bridge between the boxes.

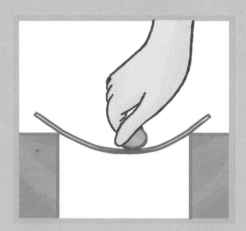

2. Test the bridge by standing the weight in the middle of it. Can a single strip of card hold the weight up?

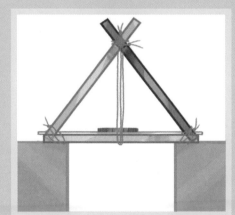

3. If not, use your other materials to try to build a bridge that is strong enough.

You could use card to make an arch to support the deck. Or see if you can build a suspension bridge with straws and string.

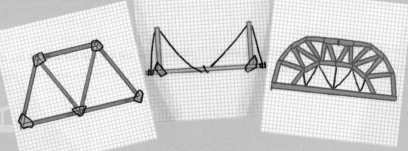

You Can Be a Prosthetist

A prosthetic is an artificial replacement for a missing body part, such as an arm or leg. A prosthetist is the expert who makes them.

Prosthetics date back to ancient times. They were especially important in periods of war, when many people lost limbs.

When Roman general Marcus Sergius lost a hand in battle, he had an iron hand made. It could hold his shield and allowed him to return to fighting.

In 1566, astronomer Tycho Brahe lost his nose in a duel and got a replacement metal one.

More recently, we've invented prosthetics that can move and work like the body part they replace.

One way to do this is to use strings that pull on parts to make them bend. This is actually what happens in the real human body, too.

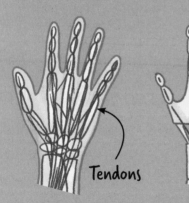

Tendons

Robot artificial hand with cord tendons

In a real hand, strings called tendons pull on the fingers to bend and straighten them.

These days, prosthetics are so good that wearers can play all sorts of sports. Among the many world-class atheletes is Amy Purdy, an American snowboarder and triple Paralympic medalist, who has two prosthetic legs.

Activity: Moving Finger

Make a bending model finger using just a few simple items you'll likely have at home.

You will need:

- Scissors
- A straw
- Ruler
- String
- Tape

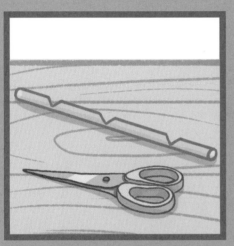

1. Use the scissors to cut three triangle-shaped notches along one side of the straw about 2–3 cm (1 inch) apart.

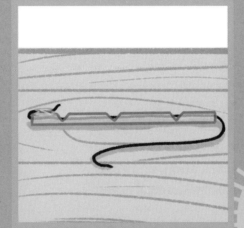

2. Cut a piece of string about 5 cm (2 inches) longer than your straw. Thread it through the straw.

Modern mechanical arm

3. Tape the string to the top end of the straw to hold it in place. To bend the finger, hold it at the base and pull the string.

Can you use the same technology to make other things? How about:
- A whole hand with 4 fingers and a thumb
- A working foot
- An octopus?

35

You Can Be a Music Maker

Like the wheel, musical instruments are such an old invention that no one knows who was the first person to think of them. Why not have a go at making some of your own?

The first instruments were probably percussion instruments, such as drums and rattles. People banged sticks and stones together to play a beat. For tunes, inventors had to figure out how tubes, sticks, or strings of different shapes and sizes made different musical notes.

4100 BCE: The flute is invented. It has holes that you cover with your fingers to blow different notes.

3200 BCE: The first lyre is made. It is a very early stringed instrument.

1000 BCE: The lur is invented. It is similar to an early bronze horn.

History is full of amazing musical instrument inventions ...

1700: Italian Bartolomeo Cristofori invents the piano.

1931: The first electric guitar is invented by George Beauchamp.

1945: Hugh Le Caine invents the first electronic synthesizer.

Activity: Make a Musical Instrument

People still invent musical instruments today, often using everyday objects. Try making this bottle organ to find out how to create different musical notes.

You will need:

- Some clean, empty glass bottles, preferably the same size
- A metal spoon
- Water

1. First, try playing the bottles. You can tap them with a spoon or blow across the top to make a soft musical note.

2. Stand the bottles in a row, and pour a different amount of water into each one.

3. Play the bottles to see what notes they make.

4. See if you can adjust the amounts of water to make a musical scale (like on a piano) or a sequence of notes that makes a tune.

You Can Make a Microscope

Microscopes have played a crucial role in many important scientific discoveries—without them, Rosalind Franklin would never have discovered the structure of DNA! The first person to make and use one was Antonie van Leeuwenhoek, a cloth trader in the Netherlands. In the 1670s, he began making magnifying lenses in order to look more closely at cloth. Imagine his surprise when he discovered a whole world of microscopic organisms!

Antonie van Leeuwenhoek's microscope

Point for holding objects

Metal plate

The lens was a tiny sphere, made by melting a thin strand of glass

Van Leeuwenhoek looked at tooth plaque, pond water, and lots of other things. He was amazed to see tiny wriggling creatures, which he called "animalcules."

Now we know that his "animalcules" were bacteria and living things.

Drawings of van Leeuwenhoek's "animalcules"

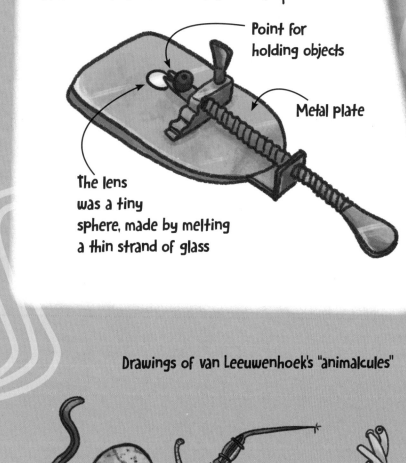

Activity: Sphere Microscope

You can make a microscope like van Leeuwenhoek's, using a drop of water instead of a glass sphere.

You will need:

- A postcard
- Scissors
- Ruler
- Foil
- Tape
- Thick needle
- Cocktail stick or wooden skewer
- Petroleum jelly or cooking oil
- Water
- Flashlight
- Objects to look at, such as onion skin or a feather

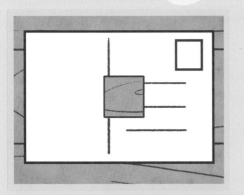

1. Cut a hole in the middle of the card, about 2-3 cm (1 inch) square.

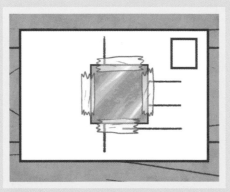

2. Cut a slightly larger piece of foil, and tape it over the hole.

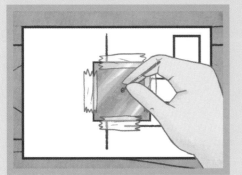

3. Use the needle to make a neat, round hole in the middle of the foil.

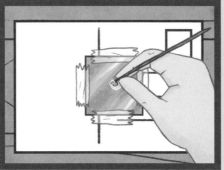

4. Dip the stick or skewer in jelly or oil, and dab some around the edge of the round hole in the foil.

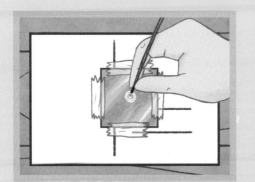

5. Dip the other end of the stick or skewer in water, and drop a drop of water onto the hole.

6. Hold the flashlight upright, switch it on, and put the object over the light.

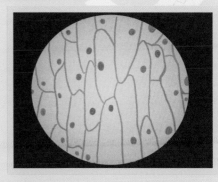

7. Hold the drop of water just above it, and look through the drop as closely as you can with one eye.

You Can Be an Architect

Some people think of art and science as very different things—even opposites. But an architect has to combine them, and be good at both.

If you like mathematics and science, but are really passionate about drawing and art, you might love being an architect!

Being artistic is important, because you have to be able to think up new ideas and make your buildings look good. But if you don't get the science and measurements right, the building won't stay up!

You have to understand the science of how buildings work, what materials to use, and how to measure everything really carefully, so it's EXACTLY right. But without creativity and imagination, your buildings could be kind of dull ...

The ideal architect has a combination of both: arty creativity and smart science skills.

Activity: Drawing a Plan

Put your measuring and drawing skills to use by making a plan of a real room. Architects draw plans like this to show the floor area of buildings and rooms.

1. Measure the lengths of all the walls and write them down.

2. Using a ruler, draw the room on the squared grid below, allowing 1 square for 1 m (3 ft) of wall.

3. Measure the positions and widths of the door and windows, and add them too.

4. If you like, you can also measure and draw in the furniture.

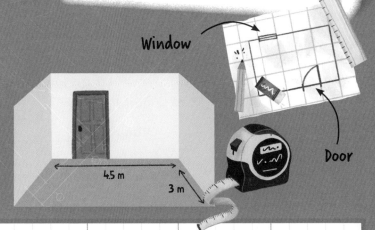

Window

Door

4.5 m

3 m

TIP: If the real room is 4.5 m (15 feet) wide, make it 4.5 squares wide on your plan.

You Can Be a Utilities Expert

Imagine you moved into your brand-new house, only to find it had no running water, electricity, or plugholes! Buildings need things like this, known as utilities.

When architects design a building, they have to think about all the utilities, and how to fit them in.

Each utility has to be carefully planned out in a detailed drawing, like this one for waste pipes and sewers.

The main utilities are water, sewers, electricity, and gas, plus phone and internet connections.

Water pipes need to lead to anything that uses water, such as showers, sinks, and toilets.

Waste pipes come out of toilets, baths, showers, and sinks into the sewers.

Electrical wires need to be connected to all the lights, light switches, and outlets.

Gas pipes need to be attached to the boiler and stove, if they use gas.

Architects also have to work with the utility providers, like water and electricity companies, to arrange to connect the building's utilities to the supplies in the street.

Activity: Utility Tangle

Neri's creating a drawing for a house she's designed, showing some of the utility systems. Now she needs to label them. One is the water supply and one is the waste water system. Then there's the electricity supply and the gas supply, too. Can you work out which lines are gas, electricity, fresh water, and waste water?

Help me work out which is which.

electricity

gas

fresh water

waste water

A
B
C
D

43

You Can Design Public Buildings

Architects design public buildings like libraries, supermarkets, malls, and law courts. They have to be easy and safe for everyone to use.

"There's a lot to think about!"

Public buildings are often paid for by local governments with a tight budget—so you'll have to manage the cost!

Your public building is there to do a job—so think about the people who will use it, and what they need.

As public buildings are often in built-up areas, they have to look good and fit in with their surroundings, too.

Don't forget fire exits, parking, cycle racks, wheelchair access, staff areas, bathrooms, and maybe a café!

The architects of these buildings had a lot to consider:

Swimming pool
- Changing rooms · Café
- Places to sit · Parking

Library
- Soundproof windows · Reading areas
- Shelving · Easy to find your way around

Supermarket
- Café · Loading bays · Bathrooms
- Parking · Storage areas

Activity: Built for Billie?

Billie is heading to town as she has a lot of things to do and people to see. It should be easy for her to go everywhere she wants in her wheelchair, but there's one building Billie will struggle to visit.

Can you identify the building that might be tricky for Billie to get into, then find it on the map?

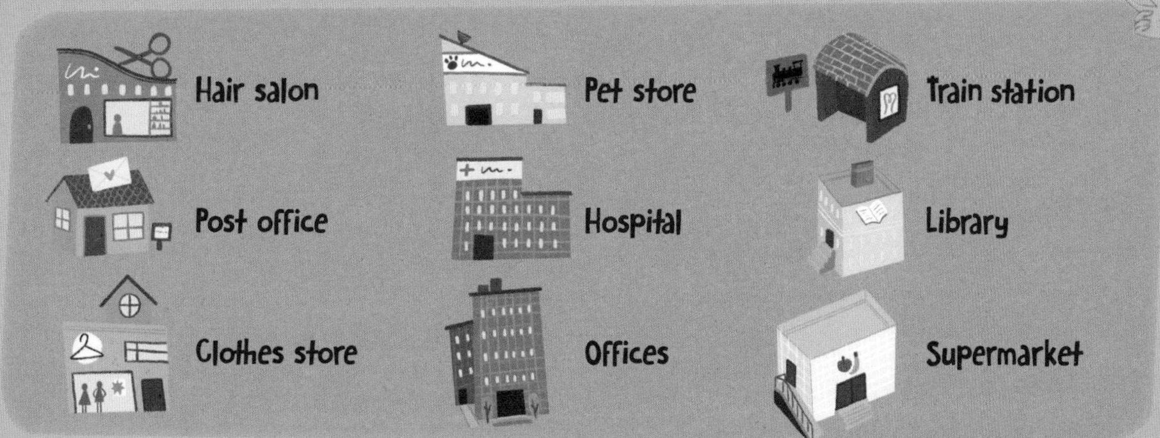

Circle the building on the map that I'll have a problem visiting.

Hair salon

Pet store

Train station

Post office

Hospital

Library

Clothes store

Offices

Supermarket

You Can Be a Town Planner

Usually, architects only work on one building at a time. But once in a while, they get to design a whole new town from scratch.

A new town, also called a planned town, is a town that's designed and built as a whole.

Most towns and cities grow gradually, adding new buildings over time. A new town is a whole new community where there was nothing before.

Governments sometimes build new towns after a natural disaster or war, or when the population increases.

Starting from scratch means architects can create a neat, regular pattern. You can see one in this plan for the new town area of Edinburgh, UK.

Edinburgh's new town isn't actually new anymore— it was built in the 1800s!

Brasília in Brazil is a famous new town. It was designed in the 1950s to be a brand-new capital for Brazil.

The architects came up with this cool design, which looks like a bird or a plane.

Activity: Twin Towns

This architect has created two slightly different new town designs for the new town council to consider.

Help the council spot the six differences. Circle them once you've found them.

Plan A

Plan B

You Can Be a Forensic Scientist

Do you want to use your science skills to solve crimes? This is what forensic scientists do. They collect evidence from the scene of a crime, and then they do tests to try to discover when it was committed and how—and who might have done it.

Think your crime-fighting skills are up to scratch? There's a lot to learn, and lots of equipment to get to grips with.

The criminal may have left traces at the crime scene—this is called "trace evidence!"

Knowledge of the human body might give us clues about the criminal.

Tests can reveal if the criminal used itching powder, explosives, or even poison!

Broken glass, splatters, and car tracks reveal how the crime was commited.

Activity: Pack Your Bag!

Before you head to your first crime scene, pack your bag. As well as equipment for collecting evidence, you need to take a clean body suit, face mask, and gloves, so you don't leave traces of yourself at the scene.

Equipment for Collecting Evidence:

- Camera
- Chemicals for tests
- Crime scene suit
- Evidence bags and labels
- Fingerprint brush and powder
- Gloves

- Magnifying glass
- Mask
- Notebook and pen
- Test tubes
- Tweezers

Which of these bags contains everything on the list?

You Can Be a DNA Detective

Cells are the tiny building blocks that make up your body. Nearly every cell in your body contains long, thin molecules of DNA. DNA contains the instructions that tell your cells exactly how to grow and function. These are passed down from parents to their children. They tell your body to have one head and a beating heart, and to have, for example, red or black hair, and brown or blue eyes. Forensic scientists can use DNA to identify people.

Since humans are pretty similar, 99.9% of your DNA is identical to everybody else's. But 0.1% of your DNA is unique to you. So, if you can find a sample of someone's DNA, you have an amazing record of that person.

DNA is the shape of a twisted ladder called a double helix.

There are thousands of rungs on each DNA ladder, giving a string of instructions.

There are around 37 trillion tiny cells in the human body.

DNA is bundled up in the nucleus of most cells.

Activity: Search for Samples!

Forensic scientists can find DNA in flakes of skin, nail clippings, and hair. They can also collect it from body fluids, such as blood, sweat, vomit, tears, earwax, pee, poop, saliva (dribble), and mucus (snot). Grab your evidence bags, and circle 5 items in this hotel room that might contain DNA samples.

You Can Track Trace Evidence

DNA is not the only trace that criminals can leave at a scene. Other types of "trace evidence" include powder from their makeup, the fluff from their sweater, or soil from their boots. If a driver has crashed into another car and sped away, there may be traces of paint from their own car.

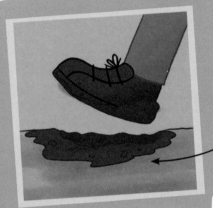

Soil can be sandy, chalky, or sticky with clay.

Soil is a mixture of grains of rock, dead plants and animals, water, and air. The exact mixture differs from place to place. Identifying the soil on someone's boots might tell us where they have been.

Soil may contain seeds or pollen from plants that grow in only one area.

Soil may be mixed with animal droppings that can be identified.

Activity: Track the Trace Evidence!

Someone has broken into the Modern Art Museum and stolen a priceless masterpiece. Examine the trace evidence found at the scene of the crime, then decide which suspect to call in for questioning.

Trace Evidence Found:

- A footprint with traces of mud and red paint
- A wisp of black yarn
- A long blond hair

The Suspects:

Suspect A is a gardener and janitor.

Suspect B is a nurse.

Suspect C is a landscape painter.

You Can Be a Virus Expert

Some microorganisms cause illness in humans. Viruses cause infectious diseases that pass from person to person, such as chickenpox. Some bacteria cause illness such as stomach upsets from eating dirty food. Some forensic scientists are experts on disease-causing microorganisms and can tell when an outbreak began.

More than 200 different viruses cause colds.

Cold viruses travel from an infected person in coughs and sneezes or in snot wiped onto objects.

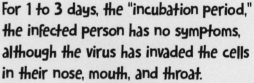

For 1 to 3 days, the "incubation period," the infected person has no symptoms, although the virus has invaded the cells in their nose, mouth, and throat.

The infected person's body fights back. Symptoms appear—sore throat, runny nose, coughing, headache, and fever—and may last 7–10 days.

Activity: Who Spread the Infection?

A burglar broke into the Infectious Disease Laboratory, breaking a vial containing the Green Spot virus and infecting themselves immediately. Seven days after the break-in, three suspects have arrived at the police station for questioning. Which suspect could have committed the burglary?

Facts About the Green Spot Virus:

- Incubation period is 3 days.
- The only symptom is large green spots.
- Spots last 5 days.
- The sufferer is highly infectious as soon as the spots appear.

The Suspects:

Suspect A
Seven days after the break-in, Suspect A has no spots, and neither do her family and friends.

Suspect B
Seven days after the break-in, Suspect B has green spots, but his family and friends do not.

Suspect C
Seven days after the break-in, Suspect C has green spots and so do her family and friends.

You Can Be a Surgeon

Sometimes, a patient needs an operation, also known as surgery, to fix something inside their body. Doctors called surgeons do operations, along with a team of other experts to help.

First, doctors have to decide when someone needs surgery. For example, if you have appendicitis, the appendix has to be removed.

If you don't mind the sight of blood and body bits, you could be a surgeon!

Other types of surgery include repairing bones, treating injuries, transplanting organs, and discovering the cause of a disease.

Surgeons carry out operations in an operating room.

The patient is covered in a cloth.

This doctor, called an anesthetist, gives the patient medicine to make sure they are fast asleep and can't feel any pain.

Nurses keep all the tools and supplies ready.

Surgeons wear face coverings, gloves, and outfits called scrubs.

Activity: Spot the Difference

An operating room is full of hi-tech machines, lighting, tools, supplies, and staff. For the surgery to go safely, everything has to be ready and in the right place.

Can you spot six differences between these two operating room scenes?

You Can Be a Heart and Lung Specialist

The heart and lungs are important organs that work together. Lungs collect oxygen from the air, and put it into the blood. The heart pumps blood around the body.

Doctors listen to your heart and lungs to check they're OK!

Stethoscope

A family doctor always has a stethoscope handy. It's a tube with a flat trumpet shape on one end, and parts that fit into the ears on the other end.

By pressing the stethoscope against a patient's chest and back, the doctor can listen to the heart and lungs.

Listening to the lungs

If you have a chest infection, the lungs might have mucus or fluid in them, and sound crackly or bubbly.

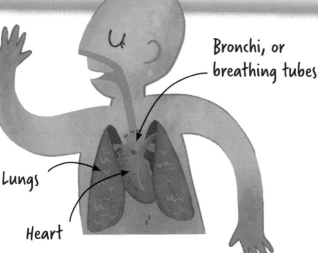

Bronchi, or breathing tubes

Lungs

Heart

When the lungs are clear and healthy, the doctor will only hear breath going in and out.

When your lungs are healthy, you can take deep breaths and blow steadily. When they're not healthy, breathing deeply can make you cough.

Hearing the heart

A healthy heart makes a regular beating sound like this:

lub-DUB!

lub-DUB!

lub-DUB!

An unhealthy heart might sound different, or have an irregular beat.

When you exercise, the heart beats faster as your muscles need extra oxygen.

Activity: Make a Stethoscope

The stethoscope is quite a simple invention! It's easy to make one of your own that really works.

You will need:

- A small, strong cardboard tube, like the tube from inside a roll of foil or plastic food wrap
- A small funnel
- Sticky tape

Ask a friend or family member if you can try out your stethoscope on them!

Push the funnel into the end of the tube.

Use sticky tape to attach it.

Press the funnel end gently on their upper chest, near the middle.

Put your ear to the other end. What can you hear?

Try it on their back too!

You Can Be an Ear Expert

As a doctor you'll have to get used to peering inside people's ears, to look for infections, ear wax, or lost objects! Doctors have a special tool for this, called an otoscope.

The hole in the ear is called the ear canal. It leads to the eardrum—a thinly stretched skin that vibrates when sound waves hit it. The sound wave patterns get passed inside the ear and then to the brain.

Ears are very delicate, which is why you should NEVER stick anything inside!

Let me look instead—it's much safer this way!

The otoscope is shaped so that it can't hurt the ear. It lights up to give the doctor a good view.

Outer ear
Some germs can infect the inside or outside of the ear, causing nasty earache.

Ear canal
People sometimes get things stuck in their ear canal.

Eardrum
A very loud noise can tear the eardrum. This really hurts!

Ear wax might seem gross, but it's useful. The wax protects the ears by trapping dust and germs. But it can sometimes build up and block the ear. A doctor will get the wax out by squirting water into the ear, or by using a special tool.

Did you know?
Different people have different types of ear wax. There are two types:

The sticky, yellowish kind

The pale, flaky kind

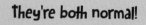

They're both normal!

Activity: Make a Model Eardrum!

This experiment shows how an eardrum works, and why it's so delicate.

You will need:

- Clear plastic food wrap
- A large bowl
- A few grains of sugar or cake sprinkles
- A loud speaker (ask an adult to help with this)

1. Stretch a piece of plastic wrap tightly over the bowl, so that it's smooth and flat.

2. Sprinkle a few grains of sugar or cake sprinkles in the middle of the wrap.

3. Position the speaker near the bowl, then play some loud music.

4. The sound should make the tightly stretched plastic wrap vibrate and the sugar or cake sprinkles bounce.

Eardrums work the same way. They only vibrate properly by being very thin and stretched. But this means they can also tear or break easily.

You Can Be a Busy Vet

Vets work with animals, of course. But a busy vet has to do a whole lot of other things as well, especially if they have their own surgery. Here are some of the things they might expect to do on a normal day.

Check out Dr. Barking's hectic day!

Seeing a tortoise for a regular check-up ...

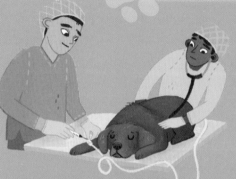

Operating on a dog that's eaten a toy brick ...

Making sure the surgery is well stocked with medicines ...

Discussing treatment options with a pet owner ...

Keeping records about all the pets she treats and the medicines she's used ...

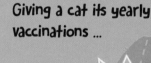

Giving a cat its yearly vaccinations ...

Managing staff, such as the receptionist and nurse.

Activity: Put It in the Diary

Dr. Barking is EXTRA busy today, and unfortunately she can't fit everything in!

Which of the tasks below do not appear in Dr. Barking's diary?

<u>Friday January 22nd</u>

8:00   Newborn pony check at Sweet Clover Farm—remember coat and boots!

9:00   Drive back to surgery for morning consultations

9:30   Rabbit medication review

9:45   Guinea pig check-up

10:00   Kitten microchipping

10:30   Dog check-up

11:00   Online training—2 hours!

13:00   Lunch break

14:00   Home visit—elderly cat

14:30   Home visit—limping dog (note—she's very nervous)

15:00   Back to surgery to interview new receptionists

18:00   Home time!

Dog check-up

Online training

Farm visit to check newborn pony

Cat vaccination

X-ray appointment

Home visit—elderly cat

Interview new receptionists

You Can Be an Emergency Vet

What happens when an animal is in a road accident, gets stuck, or is suddenly very sick? It can't wait for an appointment —you need an emergency vet right now!

I'm on my way!

Car accidents

Sadly, animals often get hit by cars. It's a big problem for pet dogs and cats who go outdoors, and for wild animals. If the vet's surgery isn't open, owners might be able to find a 24-hour emergency vet service or an animal hospital.

Extra-large emergency!

Vets also help out when whales get washed ashore and stranded on beaches. A vet can help to keep the whale calm, and advise on how to help it safely back out to sea.

In Australia, koalas are often injured in car accidents. These furry creatures mainly live in trees, and are not good at crossing roads.

So Australia has koala ambulances and koala hospitals, to rescue and treat them before releasing them back into the wild.

Activity: Which Way to the Stables?

Dr. Muddi has just got an emergency call from Abel's Stables. Their horse Abbie has fallen and can't get up. He sets off as soon as possible in his van —but what's the quickest way?

Help Dr. Muddi find the shortest and fastest route to his destination.

FINISH

START

You Can Help Stressed Animals

Vets can help animals to have healthy bodies. But their feelings matter, too! If an animal is stressed, worried, or scared, this can affect how it acts, or make it sick.

Lots of things can upset animals, and different animals get stressed about different things. For example, dogs usually don't like being left alone all day, but many cats don't seem to mind.

> A stressed pet may pee indoors, throw up, or even get bad-tempered and bite.

All these could stress out a pet:

- Loud noises, especially fireworks!
- Moving house
- Having too many people around, or new people they're not used to
- A new pet joining the household

Zoo stress

Many animals also don't like being stuck in a cage. So zoos have to keep their animals as happy as possible, by giving them large enclosures with plenty of space, places to hide, and things to do.

> Zoo vets help look after stressed animals and give them what they need to feel better.

Monkeys and apes are clever animals, and easily get bored. So zoos give them toys and activities to reduce stress.

Activity: Monkey Playpark

Zigzag Zoo is planning to build a big, brand-new enclosure for its monkeys, with plenty of toys and activities to keep them busy and happy.

What do you think it should be like? Draw your design in this space.

Here are some ideas to get you started ...

You Can Be a Dental Vet

Why don't wild animals clean their teeth? Well, because they don't have toothbrushes. But they also don't need to, because most of the food wild animals eat doesn't cause tooth problems.

But pets do sometimes get dirty teeth, which can cause tooth decay.

Dogs are especially likely to need their teeth cleaning. You can get chew toys and dog toothbrushes, but sometimes the vet has to give them a good clean.

Look at the difference!

Before cleaning   After cleaning

Vet dentists

If you really like animal teeth, you could be a dental vet. As well as cleaning, you'll have to remove broken and decayed teeth. You might visit farms and zoos, too. Looking after zoo animals' teeth can be a scary job!

Dolphins have lots of small, sharp teeth.

Dangerous animals, such as bears and wolves, are given medicine to send them to sleep first!

Activity: Whose teeth?

Different animals have very different kinds of teeth, depending on what type of food they eat.

Can you match these tooth pictures to the correct animal?

1. Fangs for catching prey

2. Small, sharp teeth for catching fish

3. Flat teeth for munching grass

4. Pointed teeth for eating meat

5. Tusks for fighting

6. Long teeth for gnawing

Dog

Horse

Bottlenose dolphin

Hippopotamus

Jaguar

Guinea pig

69

You Can Be a Paleontologist

Paleontologists study fossils. These usually form in sedimentary rock, which is made up of layers of sediment, such as mud and sand.

We can tell how old a fossil is from the rock layers it's found in. The deeper down a layer is, the earlier it formed.

Scientists can tell how old rocks are by looking at the layers. Over time, more and more sediment collects, and more and more layers form.

Scientists study the stripy-looking layers, which are called "strata."

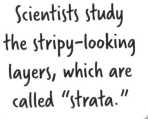

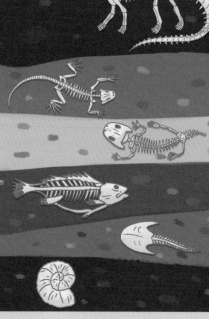

10,000 years old

500,000 years old

2 million years old

66 million years old

200 million years old

375 million years old

400 million years old

500 million years old

550 million years old

Activity: Choc Rocks

Use different types of chocolate to make an edible model of sedimentary rock.

1. Gather your materials.

2. Grate the three types of chocolate onto the three different plates.

3. Line the container with a layer of plastic food wrap.

4. Sprinkle the chocolate into the container in alternating layers of different types.

5. Cover the chocolate with the food wrap and press the layers together.

6. Unwrap the chocolate and cut it in half to reveal the layers or "strata."

You could even add candy to represent fossils as you make the different layers.

You Can Be a Dinosaur Detective

A long, long, LONG time ago, strange, monstrous creatures roamed the Earth—the dinosaurs. There are no dinosaurs alive today—they died out long before humans first appeared. Yet we know quite a lot about them, thanks to dinosaur detectives.

the dinosaurs lived from about 252 million years ago to about 66 million years ago. there were many different dinosaur types, or species—at least 700!

The dinosaur Tyrannosaurus rex

Dinosaurs belonged to the reptile family of animals, like today's lizards, crocodiles, snakes, and turtles.

Fossilized bones of a Tyrannosaurus rex

Dinosaurs are famous for growing to huge sizes, but they weren't all big. The largest dinosaur was almost as big as a blue whale, and the smallest was the size of a chicken!

We know about dinosaurs thanks to fossils—the remains, shapes, or imprints of living things from long ago, preserved in rocks.

In order to discover living things from long ago and find out more about them, scientists dig fossils out of the ground and study them. this type of science is called paleontology.

Activity: Find the Right Fossil

To start with, try matching these prehistoric reptiles to their fossilized bones.

1

2

3

4

a

b

c

d

You Can Be a Weather Scientist

So you want to be a weather scientist? There are actually many different types of weather science, and a range of different jobs you could do.

You might think all meteorologists work as forecasters on TV, but there are plenty of other jobs weather scientists can do, too.

Some meteorologists work on measuring and monitoring. They spend time outdoors, checking equipment or working with weather balloons.

Climatologists study the climate, or general weather patterns. This is extra important right now because of climate change and the effects of global warning.

Weather balloons are used to check on weather conditions high in the sky.

A climatologist might measure and compare the thickness of a glacier over time, to check if it has melted.

Research meteorologists study weather data from weather stations and satellites. They use it to work out how weather works, or to make weather forecasts.

Environmental scientists study the weather as part of the whole environment. They might study things like pollution or wildlife habitats.

This environmental scientist is testing how clean the river water is.

Activity: Spot the Difference

Weather satellites orbit the Earth, taking photos, making measurements, and tracking weather systems. They are complicated machines with lots of different parts.

Take a look at these two pictures of a high-tech GOES weather satellite. Can you spot six differences between them?

Circle six differences between the pictures.

GOES stands for Geostationary Operational Environmental Satellite.

You Can Be a Rain Expert

A lot of people don't like rain, and see it as "bad" weather. But we need it! Rain fills up reservoirs and water pipes, waters our crops, and helps plants to grow.

Rain happens when water droplets in clouds clump together and make bigger drops. When the drops are too big and heavy for the air to hold them up, they fall as raindrops.

Raindrops usually form when clouds get colder. Sometimes that's just because of cold weather. Sometimes it happens when clouds move higher in the sky, where it's cooler.

In mountainous areas, the clouds rise higher, get cooler, then drop their rain.

A rain shadow is an area that doesn't get much rain because mountains are in the way.

Rain shadow

Weather scientists usually measure rainfall in mm. They use an instrument called a rain gauge to collect the rain and see how deep it is.

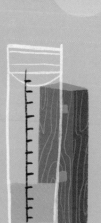

Raindrops, not teardrops!
In cartoons, raindrops are shaped like teardrops. In fact, when raindrops are falling, they are oval or burger-shaped. They only look like teardrops when they roll down a window.

Air resistance presses the raindrop flat.

Activity: Make a Rain Gauge

This simple home-made rain gauge works just like a scientific one.

You will need:
- A large, empty plastic bottle
- Scissors
- Pebbles or sand
- Water
- Ruler
- Marker pen
- Strong sticky tape

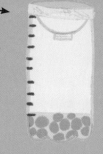

1. With an adult to help, cut the top off the bottle just below where it starts to curve.

2. Put some pebbles or sand in the bottom of the bottle. Add water to where the sides are straight, making sure the pebbles or sand are fully covered.

3. Starting from the water level, use the ruler to mark a scale up the side in cm or inches, using a marker pen.

4. Turn the cut-off top of the bottle upside down (without its lid!) and fit it into the bottle. Use sticky tape to fix the edges together.

5. Stand the rain gauge somewhere safe, outside your house or in a playground, away from walls and trees.

6. Check to see how much it fills up over a couple of weeks, and record your findings!

You Can Create Rainbows

Look—a huge, beautiful curve in the sky! In ancient times, rainbows must have seemed like magic. But now we know they're just made of raindrops and sunlight.

So how does a rainbow work? Sunlight is made up of a spectrum, or range, of shades. When light hits a raindrop, it gets reflected around inside it, then shines back out. As the light bends, the spectrum spreads out and you can see a rainbow!

Raindrops split the Sun's rays and show the whole spectrum.

Cartoons often show seven distinct bands, but if you look at a rainbow carefully you will see the bands actually blend into each other gradually.

Looks like seven bands to me!

Rare rainbows
You don't see rainbows very often, because it needs to be sunny and raining at the same time. Plus, you can only see a rainbow when you're looking at rain falling in the distance, and the Sun is shining behind you. This is why we sometimes see a rainbow after a storm, as the rain moves away and the Sun comes out.

Newton knew!
It was the great scientist Isaac Newton who decided the spectrum was made up of red, orange, yellow, green, blue, indigo, and violet.

Activity: Create a Rainbow

To see how rainbows are made from nothing but sunlight and water, make your own!

1. Stand the glass of water in a sunny place. Position the mirror behind the glass, facing the Sun.

If it's not sunny, you could try using a bright light instead.

2. Move the paper around until you catch the sunlight that has shone through the water and bounced off the mirror. You should see a rainbow appear on the paper!

Make sure you don't reflect the light into someone's eyes—that's dangerous!

You Can Understand Climate Change

Climate means the normal weather patterns in one place, or around the world. The Earth's climate is getting warmer, which is not good news!

Since the 1700s, the human population has grown a lot, and we've invented many new things, like cars, planes, and power stations. This means we've been burning more fuel, which adds polluting gases like carbon dioxide to the atmosphere. These polluting gases are also known as greenhouse gases.

Global warming is causing many problems, such as ...

• More tropical storms and cyclones

• More wildfires and droughts

• Melting glaciers

• Rising sea levels, as melted ice adds more water to the oceans

The greenhouse effect
As the Sun shines, heat and light energy enter the Earth's atmosphere. Some energy is absorbed by the Earth and some energy reflects off its surface and goes back out into space.

Energy from the Sun

Greenhouse gases trap the Sun's heat in the Earth's atmosphere, making the world warmer. This is called global warming, and deforestation, livestock farming, and landfill sites all contribute to it. We need to reduce the amount of greenhouse gases in the atmosphere to save our planet!

Greenhouse gases trap heat

Atmosphere

Polar bears need ice to hunt, but now it's melting and breaking up.

Activity: Carbon Culprits

Your friends have made a poster all about climate change, showing the kinds of things that are adding polluting gases into the atmosphere and heating our planet. Can you spot six things in the poster that contribute to global warming?

Circle six things that could be causing global warming.

You Can Be an Environmental Scientist

We humans have been polluting the air for many years with fumes from vehicles, homes, and factories. We have many ways to measure how clean the air is, or whether it needs action to clean it. One is to note how many particles (small bits of different materials) there are.

Many industries send their waste straight into the sky. Much of that waste is either tiny particles of solids, floating in the air, or gases. Both of those lead to poor air quality, which can sometimes harm people's health.

Clean air is a precious resource. The countryside is sometimes called a city's "lungs" because it gives people the chance to breathe air that hasn't been polluted. Environmental scientists aim to keep it that way.

Sensitive equipment can measure air quality. The information gathered can give us warnings about levels of air pollution.

Finland and Australia have the cleanest air. Finland is far from other countries that have large factories, and Australia is far from all other countries!

Activity: Measure Air Quality

You'd be surprised to find out how many tiny bits are floating in the air around you. But the proof is there, and you can find it by setting up these air testers in different spots near where you live.

You will need:

- Large plastic milk carton (clean and dry)
- Scissors
- Hole punch
- String
- Coin
- Marker pens
- Petroleum jelly
- Magnifying glass

1. Cut five triangle shapes from the flat side of the carton, each side about 5cm (2in).

2. Punch a hole near one corner of each triangle.

3. Cut five pieces of string, each about 20cm (8in) long, and loop each through a punched hole before tying it.

4. Trace a coin to draw a circle in the middle of each triangle.

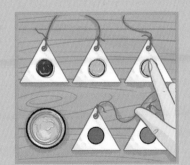

5. Shade in each circle with a marker pen and then smear petroleum jelly over the circle.

6. Hang the triangles in five different areas, such as outside your window, in a park, or by a road.

7. After three days, collect the triangles and use the magnifying glass to count the number of "bits" that each collected.

You Can Be an Ecologist

In a natural habitat, living creatures live in a delicate balance. Ecologists study how different living things interact and try to find ways to protect them from anything that might upset that balance.

A habitat is a natural region where plants and animals can live. But human activity such as uncontrolled logging or building destroys many habitats.

Habitat destruction has driven many species to extinction. More than 31,000 species are in danger of dying out soon.

Marine specialists find ways to end wasteful fishing practices that devastate marine habitats, such as bottom trawling. They are making progress, but more needs to be done.

As China's human population grows, forests of bamboo (the giant panda's main food) are lost as more buildings go up.

Quiz

Find the right answer to questions about these five endangered animals.

a. Mountain gorilla

1. These animals are threatened by hunters who break the law by selling their tusks.

b. Green sea turtle

2. These animals form huge colonies with a single queen.

3. These animals live in central Africa, but their thick fur protects them from cold weather high up in the forests.

c. Sumatran elephant

d. Bumblebee

4. This native of the Atlantic Ocean can reach speeds of 65km/h (40 miles per hour).

e. Bluefin tuna

5. Females lay up to 200 eggs in the sandy beaches of Florida and the Gulf of Mexico.

You Can Be an Environmentalist

Recycling waste helps prevent the world from becoming a mountain of trash. But what about materials that can't be recycled? Luckily, environmentalists can turn some of those into compost.

Burning trash in a landfill once seemed like an easy way of getting rid of it. But the fires create air pollution and leave behind dangerous ashes.

Environmentalists have developed compost bins that help to dispose of kitchen waste, such as vegetable peelings. It becomes a material that enriches soil.

Want some help with your home composting? Make sure you have some worms living there! Worms eat half their weight in thrown-away food ... and what they leave behind becomes rich compost.

Many local environment departments organize large-scale composting. Trucks take people's trash to a large composting unit. Residents can then share the soil-enriching finished product.

Activity: Making Compost

With a little help from a grown-up (to get started), you can start to recycle your kitchen scraps and make compost. It's really simple, and your family will be impressed with the results.

You will need:

- Black spray paint
- Large plastic bottle (empty but with the lid screwed on)
- Newspaper
- Sharp knife or scalpel
- Nail (to poke holes in the bottle)
- Shredded paper or dried leaves
- Vegetable scraps
- Eggshells
- Heavy-duty tape
- Water

1. Spray-paint the bottle in a well-ventilated area. Make sure it is completely black.

2. Have an adult cut three sides of a rectangle midway up the side of the bottle.

3. Ask the adult to poke about 12 evenly spaced holes. These will let air into your compost maker.

4. Add shredded paper or dried leaves to a height of about 7–8cm (3in).

5. Top with vegetable scraps and eggshell bits, then tape over the opening and add a little water. Set it on a sunny windowsill.

6. For the next four weeks or so, roll the bottle regularly to mix up all the ingredients.

You Can Be a Water Warrior

Think of all the water polluted because of careless human activity. Can some of it be cleaned? Yes, much of it can, and eco-scientists are constantly exploring new ways to do just that.

Household waste produces more water pollution than factories and farms. Eco-scientists spread the word that cleaner water depends on all of us.

Some of the biggest water clean-up successes have involved—or even been organized by—young people.

The polluted Cuyahoga River in Ohio actually caught fire in 1969. The US government responded by creating new laws to clean up its rivers and lakes.

New technology helps clean large amounts of water quickly. In the past, waste water would be pumped into the nearest river or lake, leading to severe pollution.

Activity: Water Filtering

Want a first-hand look at how dirty water (from a pond or muddy puddle) can be cleaned up? With some simple ingredients you can build a mini-water treatment plant.

1. Half-fill one jar with dirty pond water or muddy water from a puddle.

2. Have an adult cut a coin-sized hole in the base of the plastic cup.

3. Layer the filters or napkins in the plastic cup.

4. Fill it up about a third of the way with sand.

5. Fill the cup up to about two-thirds with gravel.

6. Fit the cup into the mouth of the empty jar.

7. Slowly pour the dirty water into the plastic cup and let clean water filter through into the empty jar.

Answers

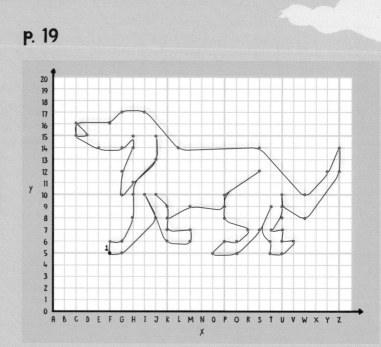

P. 7 Mostly As: You're a natural astronaut. Keep studying sciences and learning as much as you can about space, and when you're grown up, you might just be in the next class of astronauts!

Mostly Bs: You've got a lot of potential, but you might be better suited to being a space scientist who's based on Earth.

Mostly Cs: Space travel isn't for everyone, but there are lots of ways that you can be involved, so keep up your interest in all things space!

P. 11 Ready for liftoff: 1, 3, 4, 7
Safe in space: 2, 5, 6, 8

P. 15
6 x 7 = 42	9 x 8 = 72
8 x 10 = 80	10 x 6 = 60
7 x 9 = 63	7 x 10 = 70
9 x 10 = 90	9 x 9 = 81
6 x 8 = 48	6 x 9 = 54

P. 21 Circle: made up of fragments: C, G, H, O, M
Triangle: made up of fragments: A, D, F, K, N
Star: made up of fragments: B, E, I, J, L

P. 23
1. B	2. D	3. E
4. A	5. C	

P. 25 "I can read this."

P. 29 Penguin—ice-monitoring robot
Worm—soil-testing robot
Gibbon—tree-climbing robot
Gecko—wall-painting robot
Mole—robot for digging subway tunnels

P. 31 Take off
Fly forward
When you see a tree—fly right
When you see a log—fly left
When you see a log—fly left
When you see a lake—fly right
When you see an SOS signal—stop and land

P. 43 A (green)—electricity
B (blue)—fresh water
C (purple)—waste water
D (red)—gas

P. 45 The building Billie will have a problem visiting is the library, because of the steps.

P. 47

P. 49 Bag 3 contains all the necessary items.

P. 51

P. 53 It may be worth calling in Suspect C for questioning.

P. 55 Based on the symptoms of Suspect C and her family and friends, she could have carried out the break-in.

P. 57

P. 63 X-ray appointment and cat vaccination

P. 65

P. 69 1. Jaguar   2. Bottlenose dolphin   3. Horse
4. Dog   5. Hippopotamus   6. Guinea pig

P. 73 1. d   2. c   3. b   4. a

P. 75

P. 81

P. 85 1. c   2. d   3. a   4. e   5. b

Glossary

3D printing Creating a physical object from a computer model, usually by building it up from many layers.

Anesthetist A human or animal doctor who makes sure a patient is unable to feel pain during surgery.

Architect Someone who designs buildings and supervises their construction.

Artificial Made by humans, instead of occurring naturally.

Astronaut A person who is trained to travel in a spacecraft. Called a cosmonaut if they are from Russia.

Atmosphere A shell of gases kept around a planet, star, or any other object by its gravity. Earth's atmosphere is 78 percent nitrogen, 21 percent oxygen, and small amounts of argon, carbon dioxide, and other gases.

Axis The bottom or side line of a graph, along which are written the measurements.

Bacteria A type of tiny, single-celled living thing. Some types of bacteria are germs and can cause illness.

Bar chart/bar graph A diagram in which numerical values are shown by the height or length of lines or rectangles.

Binary A system of counting or notation that has 2 as its base. Referring (in coding) to the binary number system, which contains only two digits (0, 1). Binary code uses that system to program yes/no, on/off, and two-way choices.

bit The smallest unit of data in a computer, consisting of a single binary number (0 or 1).

Bronchi Large tubes that carry air into the lungs.

Budget A set amount of money to spend on a project.

Cable A thick rope used for holding up a bridge, often made of steel.

Calculator A machine used for doing mathematical calculations.

Carbon dioxide A gas found in the air, and released when fuels burn and by respiration (breathing), which helps to cause global warming by trapping heat in the Earth's atmosphere.

Cells Tiny living units that make up the bodies of humans, animals, plants, and other living things.

Chemical Any basic substance that is used in (or produced by) a reaction involving changes to atoms or molecules.

Climate The typical or average weather in a particular place, or on Earth as a whole, over a long period.

Climate change A change in Earth's climate and weather patterns, caused by increasing amounts of greenhouse gases, such as carbon dioxide, in the air.

Composting Mixing decaying leaves, vegetables, and other natural ingredients to improve soil.

Compress To squeeze and make smaller.

Coordinates A set of values that show a position on a graph.

Cord A string-like part used in some robots to make limbs move.

Cupola The observatory module of the ISS. It has seven windows used for experiments, dockings, and viewing Earth.

Cyclone A swirling windstorm around an area of low air pressure. Also used to mean a tropical cyclone in the Indian or South Pacific Ocean.

Data The information that a computer needs to operate.

Decay To rot and break down into simpler ingredients.

Decode To convert a coded message into an understandable one.

Deforestation Cutting down and clearing forests.

Desalination The process of removing salt from seawater in order to make it drinkable and useful for farming.

Digit Any of the numbers 0 to 9.

DNA (deoxyribonucleic acid) The material found in the cells of nearly all living things that controls the growth and work of cells. The instructions contained in DNA are passed down from parents to their children.

Drag A force acting opposite to the motion of an object, which restricts that motion.

Drone A flying machine without a pilot, which can be robotic, or remotely controlled by a human.

Drought A period of very dry weather that can cause water shortages and harm crops.

Dwarf planet A spherical astronomical body that orbits the Sun but is smaller than a planet and so cannot disturb other objects from its orbit.

Eardrum A thin skin within each ear that moves backward and forward very quickly when reached by sound waves.

Enclosure A cage or fenced area for a zoo animal to live in.

Energy The power to make something active.

Engineer Someone who is trained to design, build, fix, and operate machines, engines, or software.

Environment The natural surroundings of a living thing, or more widely the natural features of the planet.

Evidence Information or materials that prove whether or not something is true. Evidence can be used in a court of law to try to prove the facts about a crime.

Exoskeleton In robotics, this means a kind of robotic body suit that the wearer can control, giving them extra strength or abilities.

Extinct No longer existing, having died out as a species.

Fever An increase in body temperature, caused by illness.

Force An influence that produces a physical change or a change in movement.

Forensic scientists Experts who use scientific methods to collect and test evidence in order to solve crimes. Science is the study of natural things through careful looking and experimenting.

Fossil The remains or trace of a prehistoric living thing, preserved in rock.

Fractal A repeated geometric pattern.

Fracture A broken bone.

Fuel A material that is burned to produce heat or power.

Germ A microorganism, especially one that causes disease.

Glacier A large, slow-moving mass of ice on a mountain or in a polar area.

Global warming An increase in the Earth's average temperature, caused by increasing amounts of greenhouse gases, such as carbon dioxide, in the air.

Habitat The natural surroundings where a plant or animal species likes to live.

Humanoid A robot that resembles a human in its appearance and the ways it can move.

Incubation period The time between being exposed to an infection and getting the first symptoms.

Infection What happens when germs get inside the body, or a body part.

ISS (International Space Station) An artificial satellite that circles around Earth with astronauts living on board and carrying out scientific experiments.

Laboratory A room or building set up for scientific experiments and research.

Landfill A site, or large hole in the ground, where rubbish is piled up, then covered over.

Landslide Soil or rocks sliding or slipping down a slope.

Lens A piece of glass with one or both sides curved for concentrating or dispersing light rays.

Light year The distance light travels in one year (about 9.5 trillion km/5.9 trillion miles).

Livestock Farm animals.

Machine A piece of equipment with several moving parts. It uses power to do a particular type of work.

Magnify To make something appear bigger than it is, usually with a lens or microscope.

Meteorologist A scientist who studies weather and the atmosphere.

Microgravity Very weak gravity, the kind you would find inside a spacecraft circling around Earth.

Microorganisms Living things too small to be seen without the help of a microscope.

Microscope An instrument that uses lenses to view very small objects and living things.

Molecule A group of atoms bonded together. They form what is known as a chemical compound. A molecule is the smallest particle that still has all the chemical properties of the substance.

Mucus A slimy substance made by some body parts, such as the nose and lungs.

Multiple The result of multiplying a number by a whole number.

Multiply To add a number to itself a specified number of times.

New town A town that is designed and built as a whole from scratch.

Nucleus The "brain" of a cell that helps control its function, including growth and reproduction.

Online On the Web or Internet.

Operating room A room in a hospital, used for carrying out surgery (operations).

Operation Another name for surgery.

Orbit A fixed path taken by one object in space around another because of the effect of gravity.

Organs Body parts that have particular jobs to do, such as the brain, stomach, or heart.

Organ transplant Replacing a damaged organ with one donated by someone else.

Otoscope A special tool that a doctor uses for looking inside the ear.

Oxygen A gas found in the air on Earth that is essential for life. It is part of the atmosphere and is used for respiration. It is produced by plants in photosynthesis.

Paleontology The study of fossils and what they reveal about prehistoric life.

Particle A tiny substance, usually too small to be seen by the naked eye.

Percussion instrument Musical instrument played by shaking or by hitting (with a stick or the hand).

Planet A world, orbiting a star that has enough mass and gravity to pull itself into a ball-like shape and clear space around it of other large objects.

Pollen A powder made by the male parts of a flower. When the female parts of a flower receive pollen, they can produce seeds.

Pollution Human waste products added to air, water, or other natural substances, making them dirty or harmful.

Prehistoric From the time before written history.

Prey An animal that is hunted and eaten by another animal.

Program A set of instructions that tells a robot or other computerized device how to carry out a task.

Prosthesis An artificial body part used to replace a body part that is missing.

Proxima Centauri The closest star to Earth (except the Sun). It is a red dwarf star, much smaller than our Sun, and cannot be seen with the naked eye.

Rain gauge A device that measures the amount of rainfall.

Rain shadow A dry area next to a mountain or mountain range, where rain clouds rarely reach.

Ray A narrow stream of energy, usually of visible light, moving in a straight line.

Reptile A type of vertebrate animal that usually has scales and lays eggs.

Reservoir A natural or artificial lake where water is collected for the water supply.

Resource Any substance that is useful for human life.

Rocket A vehicle that drives itself forward through a controlled chemical explosion and can therefore travel in the vacuum of space.

Rotor A part of a machine that spins, especially the part supporting the turning blades that provide lift for a helicopter.

Rover A space exploration vehicle that carries equipment, robots, or humans across the surface of a planet or other astronomical body.

Saliva Another name for spit, the liquid the body releases inside your mouth.

Sample A small part of a substance, often used for testing.

Satellite Any object orbiting a planet. Moons are natural satellites made of rock and ice. Artificial satellites are machines in orbit around Earth.

Scalpel A very sharp knife that surgeons use to do operations.

Scrubs Clean, practical clothes that doctors and vets often wear, especially for doing surgery.

Sediment Mud, sand, or other material that settles in layers, usually at the bottom of a liquid.

Sedimentary rock Rock made of layers of hardened sediment.

Sedna A minor planet on the edge of our Solar System, three times farther from the Sun than Neptune.

Sewers Pipes, usually underground, that carry away dirty water and waste from toilets and sinks.

Snakebot A robot that is shaped like a snake and moves in a similar way.

Software The programs and other instructions used to control a robot or other computerized device.

Solar System The eight planets (including Earth) and their moons, and other objects such as asteroids that orbit around the Sun.

Sound waves Patterns of vibration, or shaking, that travel outward from the source of a sound.

Spacecraft A vehicle that travels into space.

Span The length of something from point to point; the distance on a bridge between two supports.

Species The scientific name for a particular type of living thing.

Star An astronomical body that generates light and other energy. It is made of gas and dust.

Stethoscope A medical instrument for listening to a person's or animal's heart or lungs.

Strata Layers of rock formed and laid down over time, with the oldest rocks in the lowest layers.

Streamlined Designed to increase speed and ease of movement, with reduced resistance.

Stress A difficult or upsetting situation that can make an animal or human feel unhappy or behave badly.

Surgeon A doctor or vet who carries out surgery.

Surgery (noun) A name for the building where a doctor or vet works.

Surgery (verb) Working on a person's or animal's insides to fix, mend, replace, or treat a body part.

Suspect A person thought to be possibly guilty of a crime.

Suspension bridge A bridge for which the weight of the deck is supported by vertical cables attached to other cables that run between towers.

Symptoms Changes in the body and brain caused by a disease.

Technology The use of scientific knowledge for practical purposes.

Tendon A string-like part that pulls on body parts to make them move; found in living things and in robots.

Thermal To do with heat.

Trace evidence Materials left behind while committing a crime, including hair, scraps or threads of clothing, soil, and glass.

Unique Unlike anything else.

Universe All of space and everything in it.

Utilities Services that are connected to a building, such as water, electricity, gas, phone lines, and sewers.

Vaccination Giving an animal a type of germ to help its body learn to fight off a disease.

Virus A kind of very tiny germ that works by invading body cells.

Weather balloon A type of balloon with measuring devices on it that is released into the sky to measure weather conditions.

Weather satellite A human-made satellite orbiting the Earth, used to capture images of weather patterns or record weather information.

Weather station A building or device that measures many different aspects of the weather.

Wildfire A fire burning out of control across a large area, especially in the wilderness or countryside.

X-ray A type of photo that can show a person's or animal's insides.

X axis The horizontal scale on a graph, usually read from left to right.

Y axis The vertical scale on a graph, usually read upward.

Index